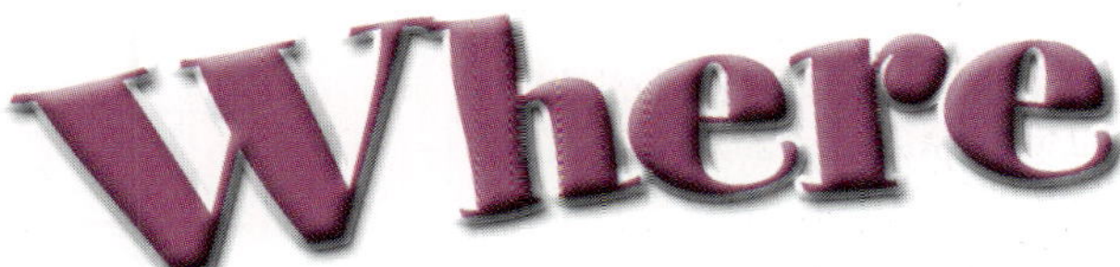

By Tony Suarez

Illustrated by Michael Weber

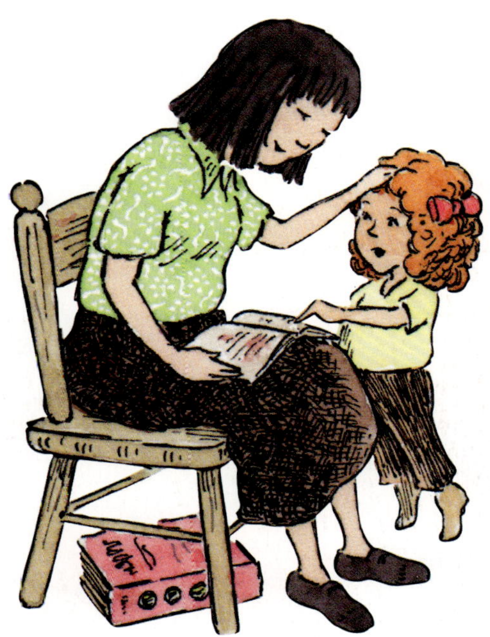

Target Skill Positions

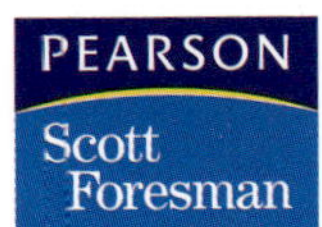

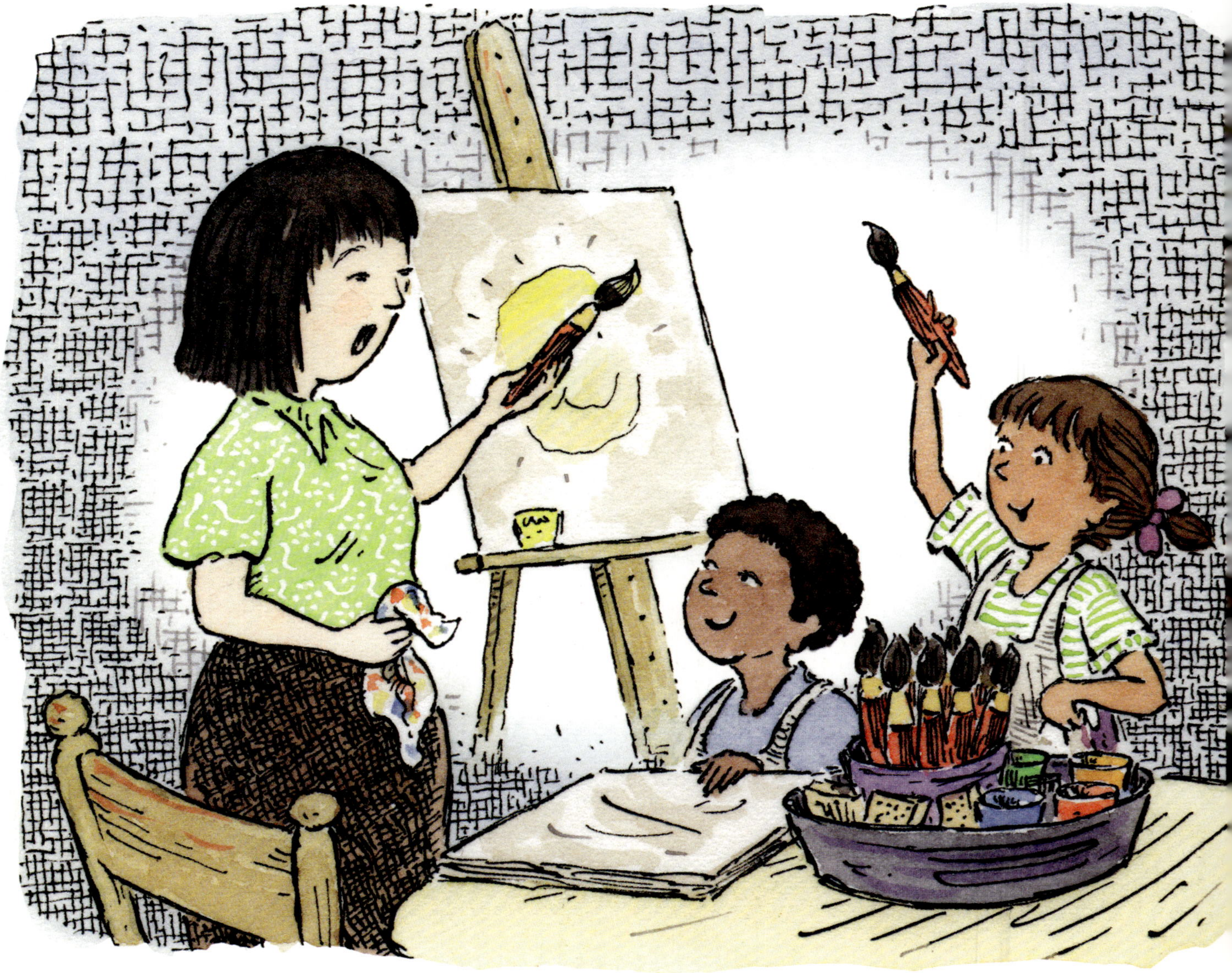

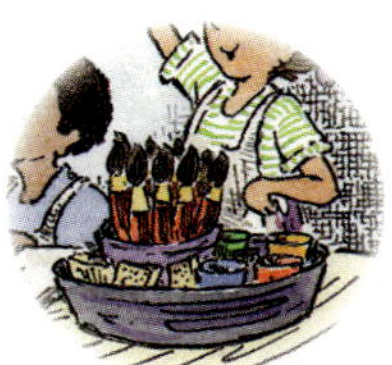

in

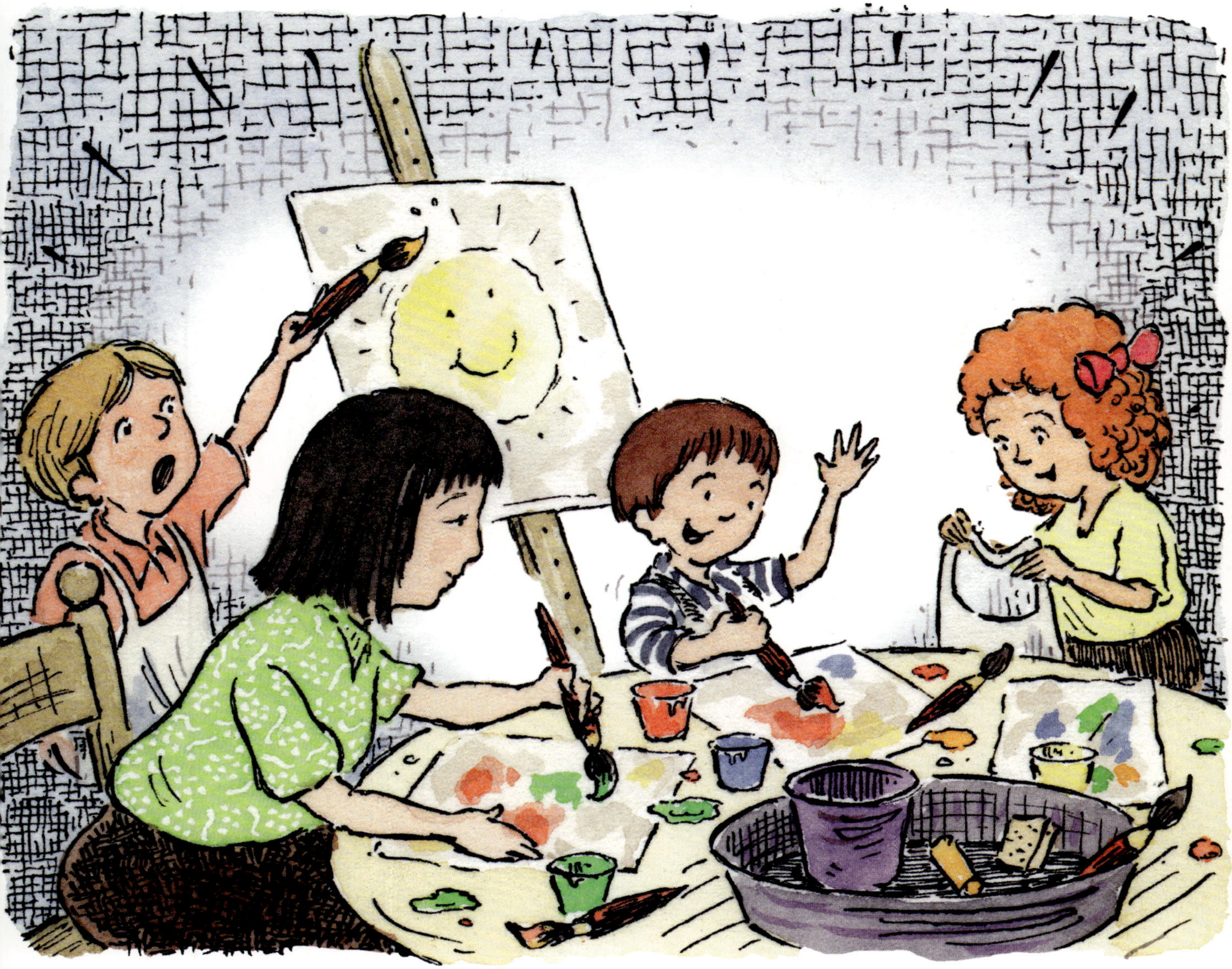

out

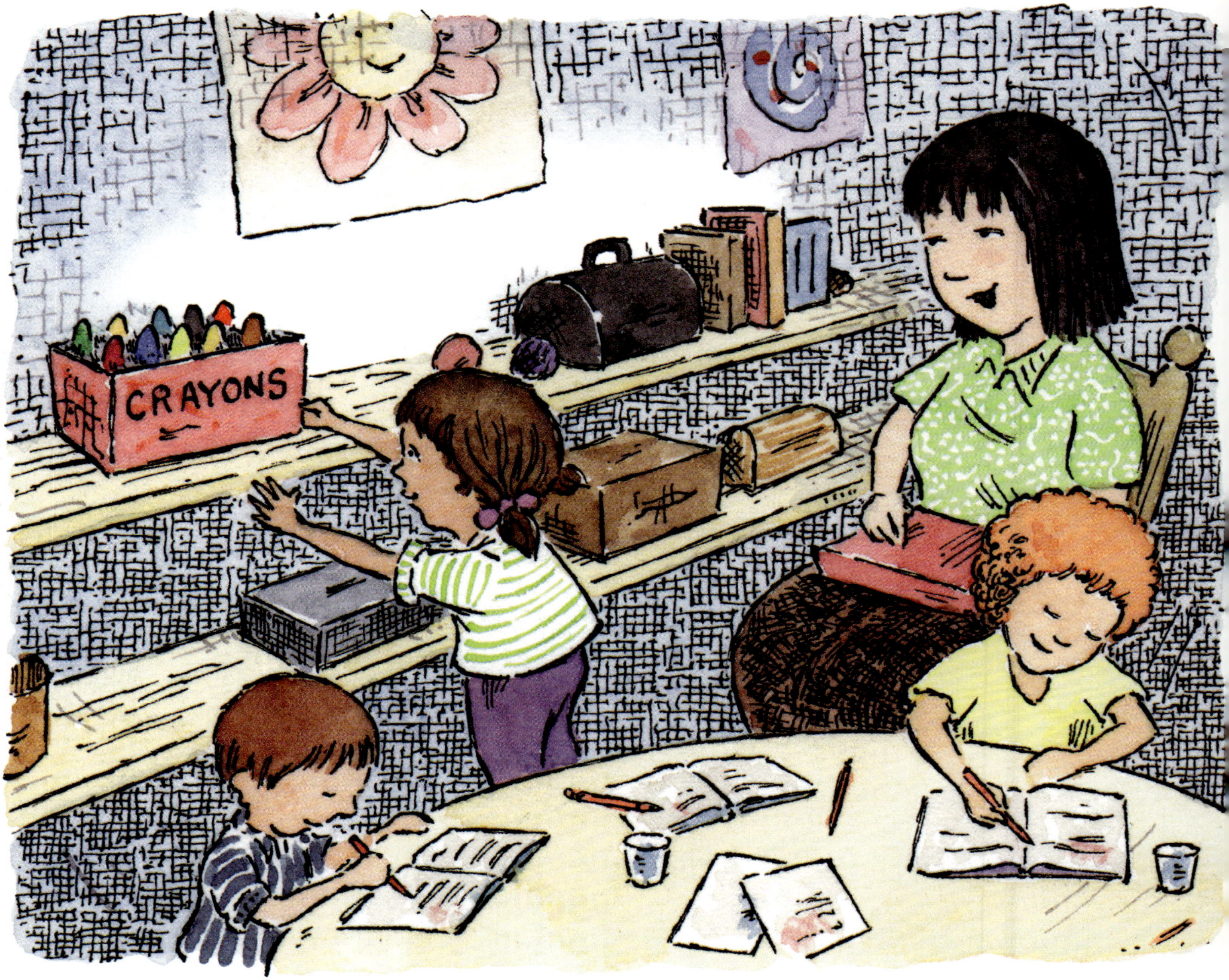

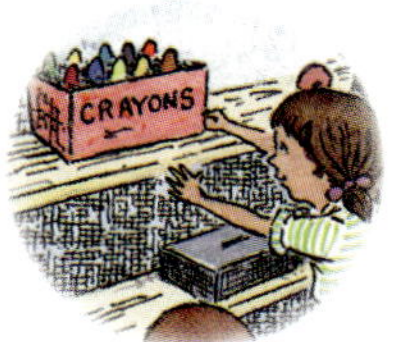

top

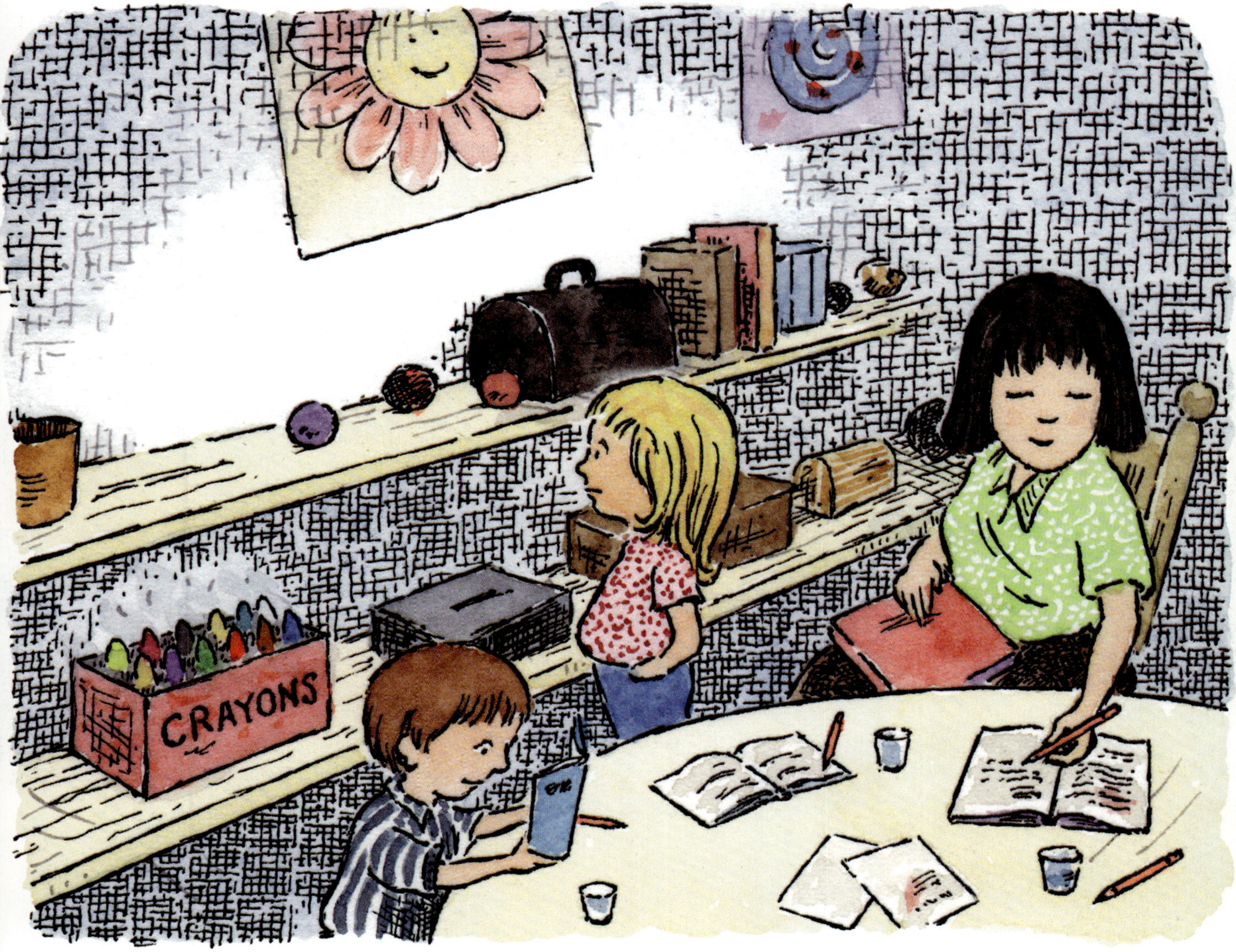

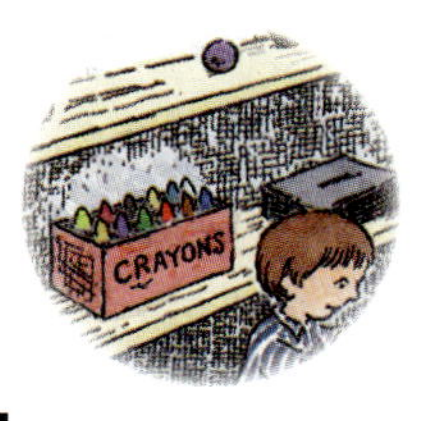

bottom

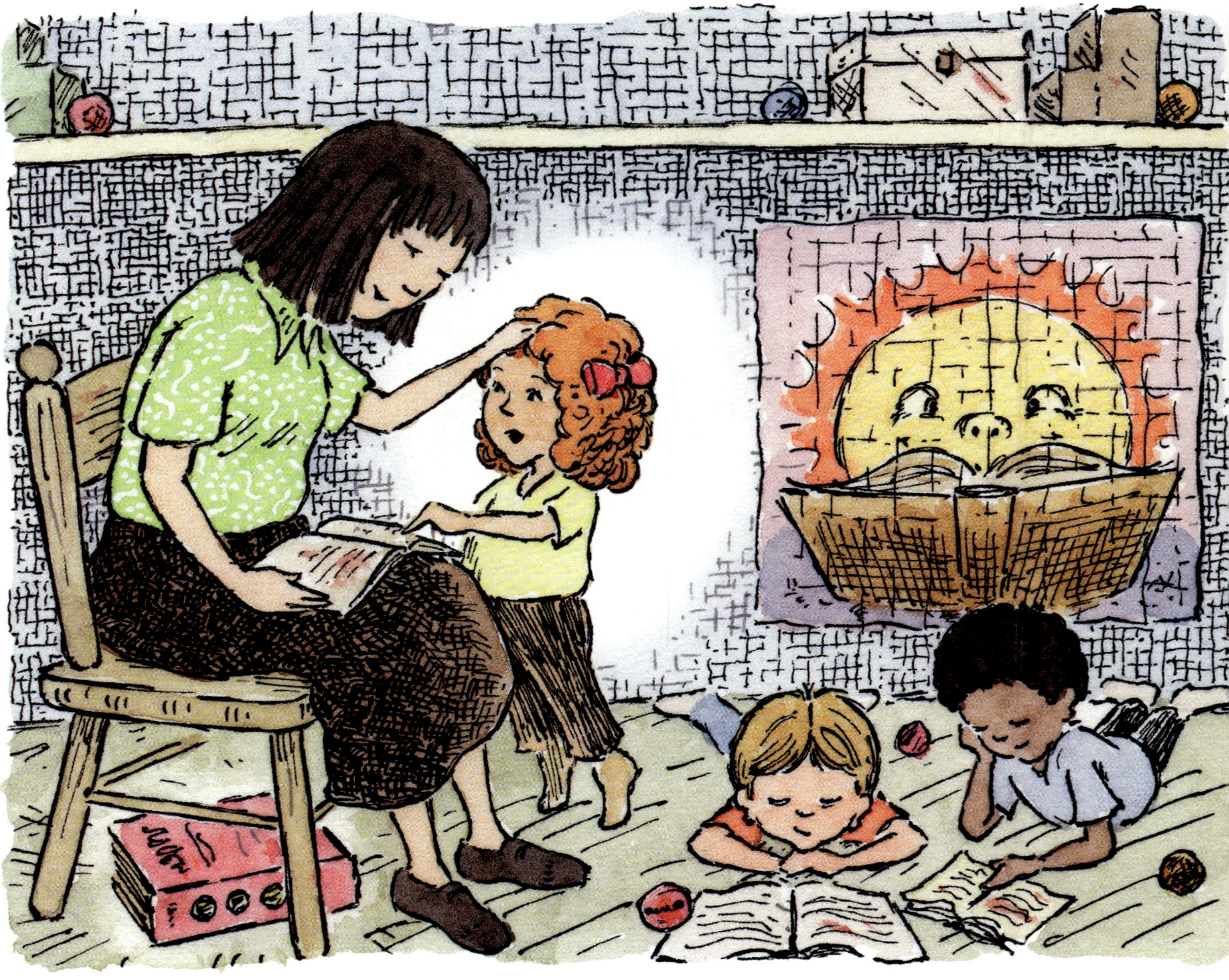

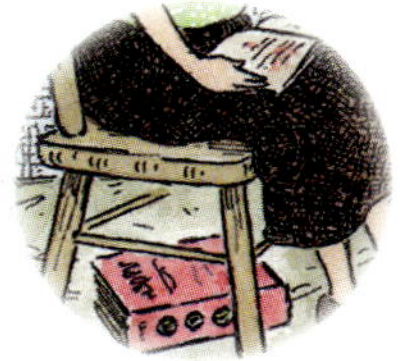

under

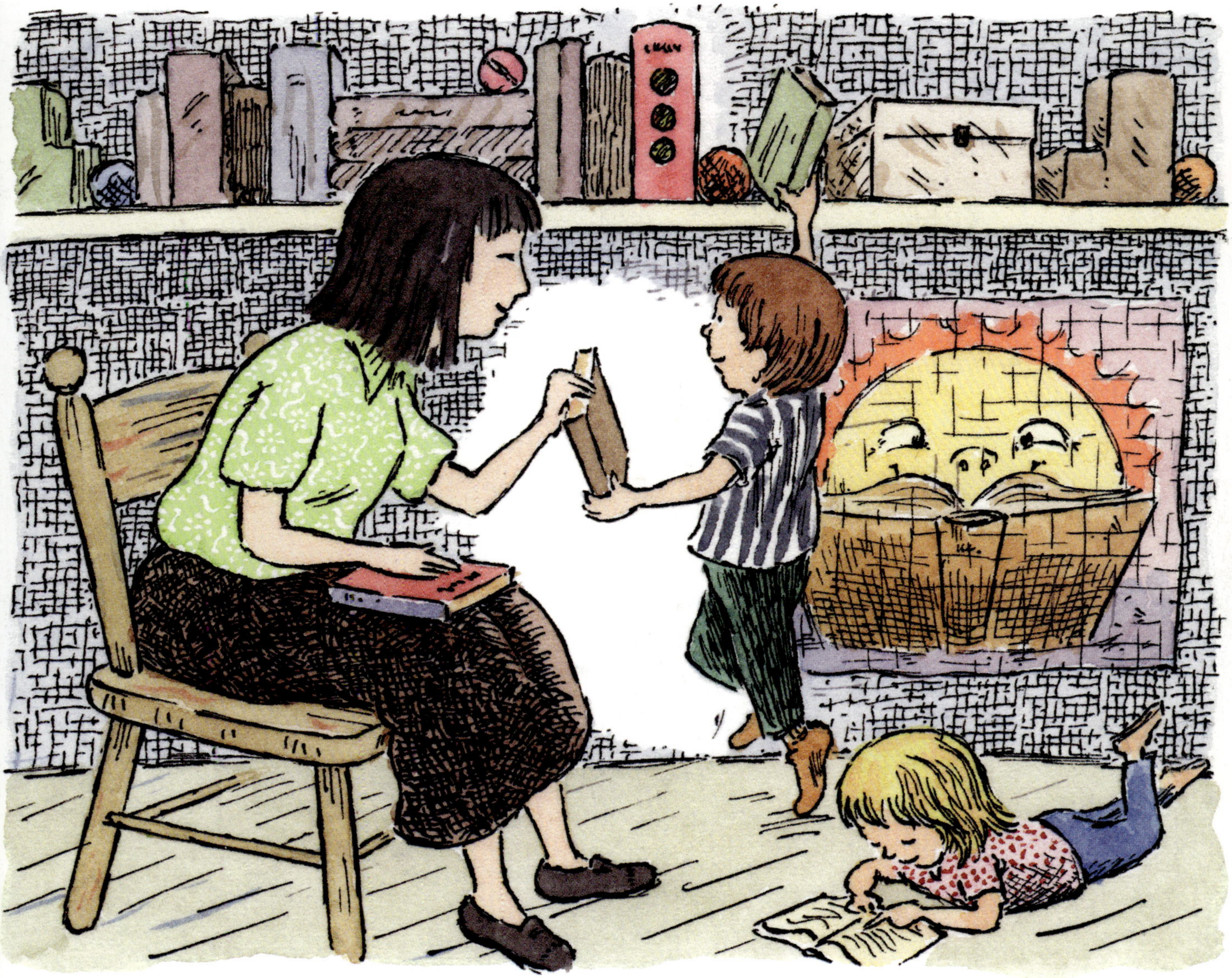

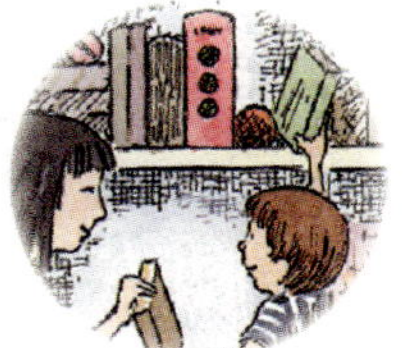

over

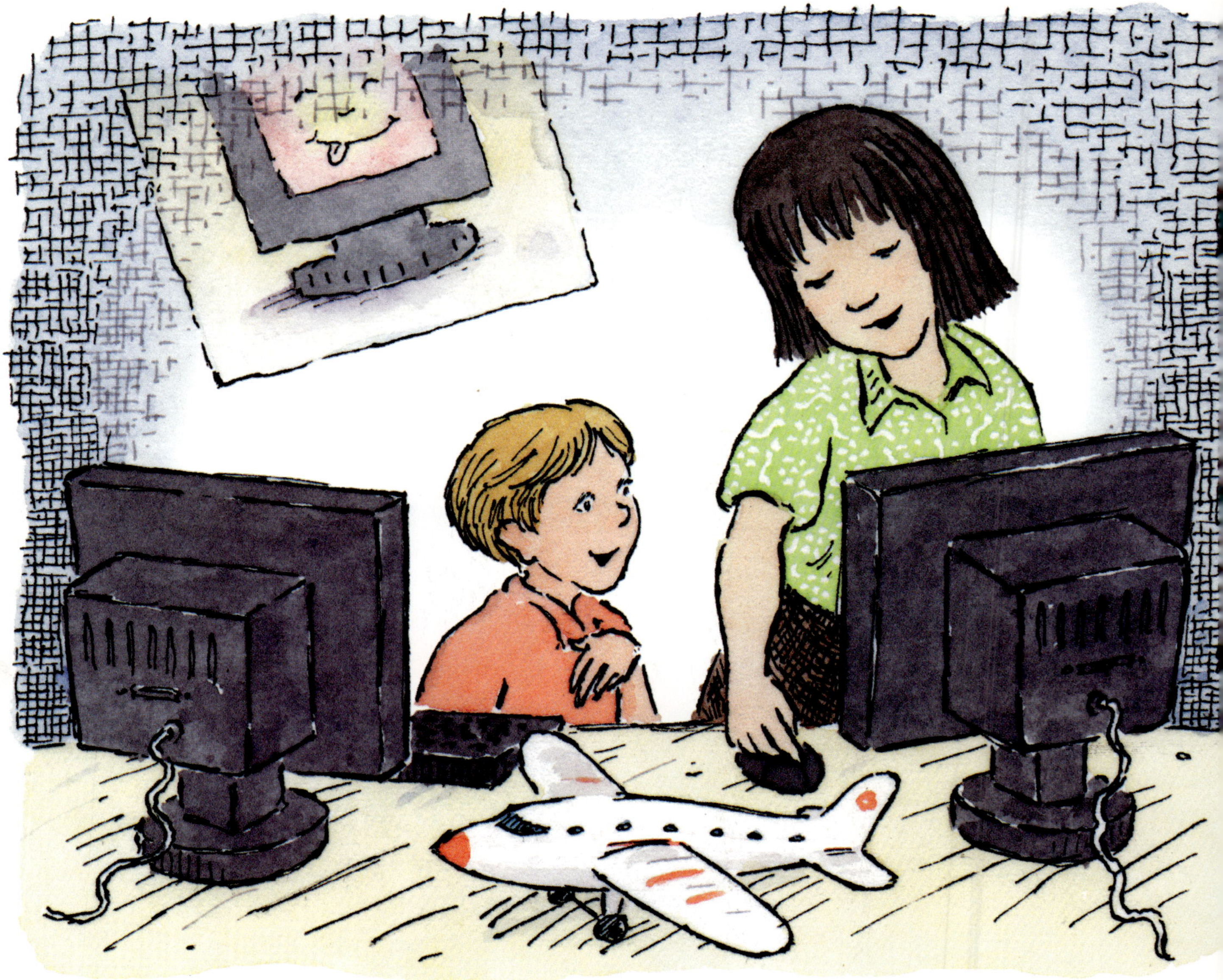

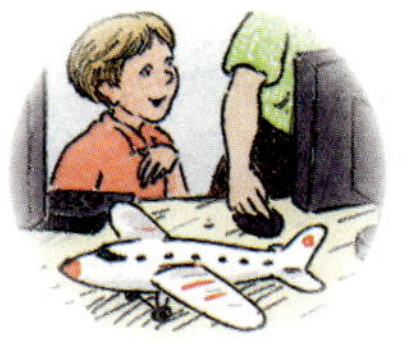

in between